Ancient Records Of The Assyrian Conquering Kings

Charles F. Horne

Kessinger Publishing's Rare Reprints

Thousands of Scarce and Hard-to-Find Books on These and other Subjects!

- Americana
- Ancient Mysteries
- Animals
- Anthropology
- Architecture
- Arts
- Astrology
- Bibliographies
- Biographies & Memoirs
- Body, Mind & Spirit
- Business & Investing
- Children & Young Adult
- Collectibles
- Comparative Religions
- Crafts & Hobbies
- Earth Sciences
- Education
- Ephemera
- Fiction
- Folklore
- Geography
- Health & Diet
- History
- Hobbies & Leisure
- Humor
- Illustrated Books
- Language & Culture
- Law
- Life Sciences

- Literature
- Medicine & Pharmacy
- Metaphysical
- Music
- Mystery & Crime
- Mythology
- Natural History
- Outdoor & Nature
- Philosophy
- Poetry
- Political Science
- Science
- Psychiatry & Psychology
- Reference
- Religion & Spiritualism
- Rhetoric
- Sacred Books
- Science Fiction
- Science & Technology
- Self-Help
- Social Sciences
- Symbolism
- Theatre & Drama
- Theology
- Travel & Explorations
- War & Military
- Women
- Yoga
- *Plus Much More!*

We kindly invite you to view our catalog list at:
http://www.kessinger.net

THE GREAT AGE OF ASSYRIA

(889–626 B.C.)

RECORDS OF THE KINGS

" Their fighting men I slew.   Their spoil I carried away,
Their cities I threw down, dug over, and burned with fire."
—A COMMON PHRASE OF THE INSCRIPTIONS.

" Hezekiah I shut up like a caged bird in Jerusalem, his royal
city."
—KING SENNACHERIB.

RECORDS OF THE ASSYRIAN KINGS

(INTRODUCTION)

ASSYRIA began to rise to military power as early as the period of the Tel-el-Amarna letters (1400 B.C.). At that time her rulers had become rivals of Babylon. But the fighting Assyrian kings met many a rebuff, and the age of their actual world-empire scarcely begins until we come to King Shalmaneser III., who ruled from 858 to 824 B.C. Shalmaneser was not, like the earlier Assyrian kings, a mere marauder, a ravager of other lands. He was a statesman, an organizer, who tried to retain permanent hold of the regions he had conquered, and to restore them to prosperity under his control. Shalmaneser III. is also the first Assyrian king of whom we know definitely that he came in contact with the kings of Bible story, the Hebrew rulers of Judah and Samaria, and the Aramaic kings of Damascus.

Shalmaneser asserts his victory over all these western kings; but when we allow for the boastful tone of Assyrian inscriptions it seems probable that they fairly held their own against him. The consolidation and extension of his power were mainly in his own valleys of the Tigris and Euphrates. Several of Shalmaneser's inscriptions have come down to us, the most noted being the one here given and known as "the black obelisk" inscription. It is engraved on an obelisk of black marble, about five feet high, which was set up in his capital. On all four sides of the obelisk there are sculptured figures of vassals bringing tribute, among them being the tribute of "Jehu of Israel," of Bible fame.

The second inscription here given is that of Tiglath-Pileser IV. (745-727 B.C.). This king carried his arms farther eastward in Asia than any other Assyrian general. The names of conquered cities on his list gradually become strange to us and we can only guess to what point he really penetrated.   Some scholars have thought he even crossed the Indus River, capturing northwestern India.

Next come the longer and still more boastful inscriptions of Sargon II. (721–705 B.C.) and his son Sennacherib (705–681 B.C.).   Both of these grim and furious destroyers ravaged the surrounding lands with a cruelty and a breadth of successful destruction previously unknown even to Assyrian annals.   Again and again Sargon II. records of a captured city, " its king I flayed " or " its warriors I set up on stakes." It was in Sargon's reign that the kingdom of Israel was finally destroyed, though the Jewish history rightly attributes the final attack to his predecessor, Shalmaneser V., who began the campaign but died before completing it.   Thus the actual destruction of Samaria, the capital of Israel, was accomplished by Sargon, and it was he who dragged the " ten tribes " of the Hebrews away to Assyria as his captives and so utterly dispersed them that we know them only as the " ten lost tribes."   Sargon in his inscription describes this capture of Samaria, its rebellion, and its second capture.

Sennacherib also tells of warring in Palestine, and boasts of his success against Hezekiah, King of Judah.   He makes no mention of the story which the Bible tells of his losing an army by pestilence; but then the Assyrian kings never mention their defeats.   We know that their campaigns were sometimes failures; but we have to read between the lines of their boasting to discover these.   Sennacherib admits quite plainly that he did not conquer Jerusalem, but only held its king besieged " like a caged bird," and then abandoned the attack, for some reason which he did not care, in his pompous record, to admit.

History knows no more astounding story than this, of these Assyrian kings marching forth, year after year, to battle.   It is tragic as it is terrible to follow any one of their records.   Each year had its campaign, and each summoned tens of thousands of men from their homes to go marching into unknown lands whence many never returned.   " Like an ibex I climbed to the high peaks against them," boasts one king, " wherever my knees had a resting-place, I sat down on a rock." And again, "my unrelenting warriors entered with weariness into their narrow passes." The peoples of these far lands were harried, slain with torture "for the honor of the great god Ashur." Their homes were destroyed; and if the next year any of them ventured to lift their heads above despair, they were crushed again. There seemed no limit to Assyria's savagery; no interest for her kings except in heaping up piles of human heads. Theirs was the military spirit gone mad. Mankind may well read and ponder on these empty boasts of " glory."

THE BLACK OBELISK OF SHALMANESER III.

FACE A

Ashur, the great Lord, the King of all
the great gods; Anu, King of the spirits of heaven
and the spirits of earth, the god, Lord of the world; Bel,
the Supreme, Father of the gods, the Creator;
5 Hea, King of the deep, determiner of destinies,
the King of crowns, drinking in brilliance;
Rimmon, the crowned hero, Lord of canals; the Sun-
god,
the Judge of heaven and earth, the urger on of all;
Marduk, Prince of the gods, Lord of battles; Adar, the
terrible,
10 Lord of the spirits of heaven and the spirits of earth,
the exceeding strong god; Nergal,
the powerful god, King of the battle; Nabu, the bearer
of the high scepter,
the god, the Father above; Beltis, the wife of Bel,
mother of the great gods;
Ishtar, sovereign of heaven and earth, who the face
of heroism perfectest;
the great gods, determining destinies, making great my
kingdom.
15 I am Shalmaneser, King of multitudes of men, prince
and hero of Ashur, the strong King,
King of all the four zones of the Sun and of multitudes
of men, the marcher over
the whole world; Son of Ashur-natsir-pal, the supreme
hero, who his heroism over the gods
has made good and has caused all the world to kiss his
feet;

FACE B

the noble offspring of Tiglath-Adar

20 who has laid his yoke upon all lands hostile to him, and
    has swept them like a whirlwind.
At the beginning of my reign, when on the throne
of royalty mightily I had seated myself, the chariots
of my host I collected.   Into the lowlands of the coun-
    try of 'Sime'si

25 I descended.   The city of Aridu, the strong city
of Ninni, I took.   In my first year
the Euphrates in its flood I crossed.   To the sea of
    the setting sun (the Mediterranean)
I went.   My weapons on the sea I rested.   Victims
for my gods I took (for sacrifice).   To mount Amanus
    I went up.

30 Logs of cedar-wood and pine-wood I cut.   To
the country of Lallar I ascended.   An image of my
    Royalty in the midst of it I erected.
In my second year to the city of Tel-Barsip I ap-
    proached.   The cities
of Akhuni, the son of Adin I captured.   In his city I
    shut him up.   The Euphrates
in its flood I crossed.   The city of Dabigu, a choice
    city of the Hittites,

35 together with the cities which were dependent upon it,
    I captured.   In my third year Akhuni,
the son of Adin, from the face of my mighty weapons
    fled, and the city of Tel-Barsip,

FACE C

his royal city, he fortified.   The Euphrates I crossed.
The city unto Assyria I restored.   I took it.   The
    town which is on the farther side
of the Euphrates, which is upon the river 'Sagurri,
    which the Kings

40 of the Hittites call the city of Pitru,[1]

<hr>

[1] Pethor in the Old Testament.

for myself I took.   At my return

into the lowlands of the country of Alzi I descended.
The country of Alzi I conquered.

The countries of Dayaeni and Elam, and the city of
Arzascunu, the royal city

of Arame, of the country of the Armenians, the country
of Gozan and the country of Khupuscia.

45 During the eponymy of Dayan-Ashur, from the city of
Nineveh I departed.   The Euphrates

in its upper part I crossed.   After Akhuni, the son of
Adin, I went.

The heights on the banks of the Euphrates as his stronghold he made.

The mountains I attacked, I captured.   Akhuni with
his gods, his chariots,

his horses, his sons, and his daughters I carried away.
To my city Ashur

50 I brought them.   In that same year the country of
Kullar I crossed.   To the country of Zamua

of Bit-Ani I went down.   The cities of Nigdiara of the
city of the Idians

and Nigdima I captured.   In my fifth year, to the
country of Kasyari I ascended.

The strongholds I captured.   Elkhitti, of the Serui-
ans, in his city I shut up.   His tribute

to a large amount I received.   In my sixth year, to the
cities on the banks of the river Balikh

FACE D

55 I approached.   Gi'ammu, their governor, they had
slain,

To the city of Tel-abil-akhi I descended.

The Euphrates in its upper part I crossed.

The tribute of the Kings of the Hittites,

all of them I received.   In those days Bir-idri [2]

60 of Damascus, Irkhulina of Hamath, and the Kings

[2] This is the Ben-hadad of Scripture.

of the Hittites and of the sea-coasts to the forces of
    each other

trusted, and to make war and battle

against me came.   By the command of Ashur, the great
    lord, my lord,

with them I fought.   A destruction of them I made.

65 Their chariots, their war-carriages, their war-material [3]
    I took from them.

20,500 of their fighting men with arrows I slew.

In my seventh year, to the cities of Khabini, of the
    city of Tel-Abni, I went.

The city of Tel-Abni, his stronghold, together with the
    cities which were dependent on it, I captured.

To the head of the river, the springs of the Tigris, the
    place where the waters rise,[4] I went.

70 The weapons of Ashur in the midst of it I rested.   Sac-
    rifices for my gods I took.   Feasts and rejoicing

I made.   An image of my Royalty of large size I con-
    structed.   The laws of Ashur my Lord, the rec-
    ords

of my victories, whatsoever in the world I had done, in
    the midst of it I wrote.   In the middle of the
    country I set it up.

FACE A, BASE

In my eighth year, Marduk-suma-iddin, King of Kar-
    Duniash,[5]

did Marduk-bila-yu'sate his foster-brother against him
    rebel;

75 strongly had he fortified the land.   To exact punish-
    ment [6]

against Marduk-suma-iddin I went.   The city of the
    waters of the Dhurnat [7] I took.

---

[3] Or, "furniture of battle."

[4] Or, "the place of the exit of the waters situated."   The tablet is
still to be seen near the town of Egil.

[5] That is, Babylon.

[6] Or, "to return benefits."

[7] The Tornadotus of classical geographers.

In my ninth campaign, a second time to the land of Akkad I went.

The city of Gana-nate I besieged. Marduk-bila-y'sate exceeding fear

of Ashur and Marduk overwhelmed, and to save his life to

80 the mountains he ascended. After him I rode. Marduk-bila-yu'sate and the officers,

the rebels [8] who were with him, with arrows I slew. To the great fortresses

I went. Sacrifices in Babylon, Borsippa, and Cuthah I made.

Thanksgivings to the great gods I offered up. To the country of Kaldu [9] I descended. Their cities I captured.

The tribute of the Kings of the country of Kaldu I received. The greatness of my arms as far as the sea overwhelmed.

85 In my tenth year, for the eighth time the Euphrates I crossed. The cities of 'Sangara of the city of the Carchemishians I captured.

To the cities of Arame I approached. Arne, his royal city, with 100 of his other towns I captured.

In my eleventh year, for the ninth time the Euphrates I crossed. Cities to a countless number I captured. To the cities of the Hittites

of the land of the Hamathites I went down. Eighty-nine cities I took. Bir-idri of Damascus and twelve of the Kings of the Hittites

with one another's forces strengthened themselves. A destruction of them I made. In my twelfth campaign, for the tenth time the Euphrates I crossed.

90 To the land of Pagar-khubuna I went. Their spoil I carried away. In my thirteenth year, to the country of Yaeti I ascended.

---

8 Or, "the Lord of sin."   9 Sumer.

Their spoil I carried away. In my fourteenth year, the
country I assembled; the Euphrates I crossed.
Twelve Kings against me had come.

I fought. A destruction of them I made. In my fifteenth year, among the sources of the Tigris and the
Euphrates I went. An image

of my Majesty in their hollows I erected. In my six-
teenth year, the waters of the Zab I crossed. To
the country of Zimri

I went. Mardak-mudammik, King of the land of
Zimru, to save his life the mountains ascended.
His treasure,

95 his army, and his gods to Assyria I brought. Yan'su,
son of Khanban, to the kingdom over them I
raised.

FACE B, BASE

In my seventeenth year, the Euphrates I crossed. To
the land of Amanus I ascended. Logs

of cedar I cut. In my eighteenth year, for the six-
teenth time the Euphrates I crossed. Hazael,

of Damascus, to battle came. 1,221 of his chariots, 470
of his war-carriages with

his camp I took from him. In my nineteenth campaign,
for the eighteenth [10] time the Euphrates I crossed.
To the land of Amanus

100 I ascended. Logs of cedar I cut. In my twentieth
year, for the twentieth time the Euphrates

I crossed. To the land of Kahue I went down. Their
cities I captured. Their spoil

I carried off. In my twenty-first campaign, for the
twenty-first time the Euphrates I crossed. To the
cities

of Hazael of Damascus I went. Four of his fortresses
I took. The tribute of the Tyrians,

[10] The King counts his passage of the river on his return from Syria
the seventeenth time of his crossing the Euphrates.

The Zidonians, and the Gebalites I received. In my
    twenty-second campaign, for the twenty-second
    time the Euphrates
105 I crossed. To the country of Tabalu [11] I went down.
    In those days as regards the twenty-four
Kings of the country of Tabalu their wealth I received.
    To conquer
the mines of silver, of salt, and of stone for sculpture I
    went. In my twenty-third year
the Euphrates I crossed. The city of Uetas, his strong
    city,
which belonged to Lalla, of the land of the Milidians,
    I captured. The Kings of the country of Ta-
    balu
110 had set out. Their tribute I received. In my twenty-
    fourth year, the lower Zab
I crossed. The land of Khalimmur I passed through.
    To the land of Zimru
I went down. Yan'su King, of the Zimri, from the face
of my mighty weapons fled and, to save his life,
ascended the mountains. The cities of 'Sikhisatakh,
    Bit-Tamul, Bit-Sacci,
115 and Bit-Sedi, his strong cities, I captured. His fight-
    ing men I slew.
His spoil I carried away. The cities I threw down, dug
    up, and with fire burned.
The rest of them to the mountains ascended. The peaks
    of the mountains
I attacked, I captured. Their fighting men I slew.
    Their spoil and their goods
I caused to be brought down. From the country of
    Zimru I departed. The tribute of twenty-seven
    Kings
120 of the country of Par'sua [12] I received. From the
    country of Par'sua I departed. To

[11] The Tubal of the Old Testament, and Tibareni of classical geographers.
[12] The Parthia of classical authors.

the strongholds of the country of the Amadai,[13] and the
   countries of Arazias and Kharkhar I went down.
The cities of Cua-cinda, Khazzanabi, Ermul,
and Cin-ablila, with the cities which were dependent on
   them, I captured. Their fighting men

FACE C, BASE

I slew. Their spoil I carried away. The cities I threw
   down, dug up, and burned with fire. An image of
   my Majesty
125 in the country of Kharkhar I set up. Yan'su, son of
   Khaban, with his abundant treasures,
his gods, his sons, his daughters, his soldiers in large
   numbers I carried off. To Assyria I brought
   them. In my twenty-fifth campaign,
the Euphrates at its flood I crossed. The tribute of the
   Kings of the Hittites, all of them, I received.
   The country of Amanus
I traversed. To the cities of Cati, of the country of the
   Kahuians, I descended. The city of Timur, his
   strong city,
I besieged, I captured. Their fighting men I slew. Its
   spoil I carried away. The cities to a countless
   number I threw down, dug up,
130 and burned with fire. On my return, the city of Maru,
   the strong city of Arame, the son of Agu'si,
as a possession for myself I took. Its entrance-space I
   marked out. A palace, the seat of my Majesty, in
   the middle of it I founded.
In my twenty-sixth year, for the seventh time the country of the Amanus I traversed. For the fourth
   time, to the cities of Cati
of the country of the Kahuians I went. The city of
   Tanacun, the strong city of Tulca, I approached.
   Exceeding fear

[13] These seem to be the Madai or Medes of later inscriptions. This
is the first notice that we have of them. It will be observed that they
have not yet penetrated into Media but are still eastward of the
Parthians.

of Ashur my lord overwhelmed him and when he had come out my feet he took. His hostages I took. Silver, gold,

135 iron, oxen, and sheep, as his tribute I received. From the city of Tanacun I departed. To the country of Lamena

I went. The men collected themselves. An inaccessible mountain they occupied. The peak of the mountain I assailed,

I took. Their fighting men I slew. Their spoil, their oxen, their sheep, from the midst of the mountain I brought down.

Their cities I threw down, dug up, and burned with fire. To the city of Khazzi I went. My feet they took. Silver and gold,

their tribute, I received. Cirri, the brother of Cati, to the sovereignty over them

140 I set. On my return to the country of Amanus I ascended. Beams of cedar I cut,

I removed, to my city Ashur [14] I brought. In my twenty-seventh year the chariots of my armies I mustered. Dayan-Ashur,

the Tartan,[15] the commander of the wide-spreading army, at the head of my army to the country of Armenia I urged,

I sent. To Bit-Zamani he descended. Into the low ground to the city of Ammas he went down. The river Arzane he crossed.

'Seduri, of the country of the Armenians, heard, and to the strength of his numerous host

145 he trusted; and to make conflict and battle against me he came. With him I fought.

A destruction of him I made. With the flower of his youth his broad fields I filled. In my twenty-eighth year,

---

[14] The Ellasar of Genesis, now Kalah Shergat.
[15] *Turtanu* ("chief prince") in Assyrian.

when in the city of Calah I was stopping, news had been brought me, that men of the Patinians

Lubarni their lord had slain, and 'Surri, who was not heir to the throne to the kingdom, had raised.

Dayan-Ashur, the Tartan, the commander of the wide-spreading army at the head of my host and my camp,

150 I urged, I sent. The Euphrates in its flood he crossed. In the city of Cinalua, his royal city,

a slaughter he made. As for 'Surri, the usurper, exceeding fear of Ashur my lord

overwhelmed him, and the death of his destiny he went. The men of the country of the Patinians, from before the sight of my mighty weapons,

FACE D, BASE

fled, and the children of 'Surri, together with the soldiers, the rebels, whom they had taken, they delivered to me.

Those soldiers on stakes I fixed. 'Sa'situr of the country of Uzza my feet took. To the kingdom

155 over them I placed him. Silver, gold, lead, bronze, iron, and horns of wild bulls to a countless number I received.

An image of my Majesty of great size I made. In the city of Cinalua, his royal city, in the temple of his gods I set it up. In

my twenty-ninth year my army and camp I urged, I sent. To the country of Cirkhi [16] I ascended. Their cities I threw down,

dug up, and burned with fire. Their country like a thunderstorm I swept. Exceeding

fear over them I cast. In my thirtieth year, when in the city of Calah I was stopping, Dayan-Ashur,

160 the Tartan, the commander of the wide-spreading army,

[16] The mountainous country near the sources of the Tigris.

VOL. I.—24.

at the head of my army I urged, I sent. The river Zab

he crossed. To the midst of the cities of the city of Khupusca he approached. The tribute of Datana,

of the city of the Khupuscians, I received. From the midst of the cities of the Khupuscians

I departed.[17] To the midst of the cities of Maggubbi, of the country of the Madakhirians, he approached. The tribute

I received. From the midst of the cities of the country of the Madakhirians he departed. To the midst of the cities of Udaci,

165 of the country of the Mannians, he approached. Udaci, of the country of the Mannians, from before the sight of my mighty weapons

fled, and the city of Zirta, his royal city, he abandoned. To save his life he ascended the mountains.

After him I pursued. His oxen, his sheep, his spoil, to a countless amount I brought back. His cities

I threw down, dug up, and burned with fire. From the country of the Mannians [18] he departed. To the cities of Sulu'sunu, of the country of Kharru,

he approached. The city of Mairsuru, his royal city, together with the cities which depended on it, he captured. To Sulu'sunu

170 together with his sons mercy I granted. To his country I restored him. A payment and tribute of horses I imposed.

My yoke upon him I placed. To the city of Surdira he approached. The tribute of Arta-irri,

of the city of the Surdirians, I received. To the country of Par'sua [19] I went down. The tribute of the Kings

of the country of Par'sua I received. As for the rest of the country of Par'sua which did not reverence Ashur, its cities

---

[17] That is in the person of his commander-in-chief, Dayan-Ashur.
[18] The modern Van.   [19] Parthia.

I captured. Their spoil, their plunder to Assyria I
brought. In my thirty-first year, the second time,
the cyclical-feast

175 of Ashur and Rimmon I had inaugurated.[20] At the
time while I was stopping in the city of Calah,
Dayan-Ashur,

the Tartan, the commander of my wide-spreading army,
at the head of my army and my camp I urged, I
sent.

To the cities of Data, of the country of Khupusca, he
approached. The tribute I received.

To the city of Zapparia, a stronghold of the country of
Muzatsira, I went. The city of Zapparia, together
with

forty-six cities of the city of the Muzatsirians, I captured. Up to the borders of the country of the
Armenians

180 I went. Fifty of their cities I threw down, dug up, and
burned with fire. To the country of Guzani [21] I
went down. The tribute

of Upu, of the country of the Guzanians, of the country
of the Mannians, of the country of the Buririans,
of the country of the Kharranians,[22]

of the country of the Sasganians, of the country of the
Andians,[23] and of the country of the Kharkhanians,
oxen, sheep, and horses

trained to the yoke I received. To the cities of the
country of . . . I went down. The city of Perria

and the city of Sitivarya, its strongholds, together with
twenty-two cities which depended upon it, I threw
down, dug up,

[20] This refers to his assuming the eponymy a second time after completing a reign of thirty years. At this period the Assyrian kings
assumed the eponymy on first ascending the throne, and the fact that
Shalmaneser took the same office again in his thirty-first year shows
that a cycle of thirty years was in existence.

[21] The Gozan of the Old Testament.

[22] Haran or Harran in the Old Testament; called Carrhæ by the
classical geographers.

[23] Andia was afterward incorporated into Assyria by Sargon.

185 and burned with fire.   Exceeding fear over them I cast.
   To the cities of the Parthians he went.
   The cities of Bustu, Sala-khamanu, and Cini-khamanu,
      fortified towns, together with twenty-three cities
   which depended upon them, I captured.   Their fight-
      ing-men I slew.   Their spoil I carried off.   To the
      country of Zimri I went down.
   Exceeding fear of Ashur and Marduk overwhelmed
      them.   Their cities they abandoned.   To
   inaccessible mountains they ascended.   Two hundred
      and fifty of their cities I threw down, dug up, and
      burned with fire.
190 Into the low ground of Sime'si, at the head of the coun-
      try of Khalman, I went down.

THE EPIGRAPHS ACCOMPANYING THE SCULPTURES

   i The tribute of 'Su'a, of the country of the Guzanians:
      silver, gold, lead, articles of bronze, scepters for the
      King's hand, horses, and camels with double backs:
      I received

   ii The tribute of Jehu, of the land of Omri, silver, gold,
      bowls of gold, vessels of gold, goblets of gold,
      pitchers of gold, lead, scepters for the King's hand,
      and staves: I received.

   iii The tribute of the country of Muzri:[24] camels with
      double backs, an ox of the river 'Saceya,[25] horses,
      wild asses, elephants, and apes: I received.

   iv The tribute of Marduk-pal-itstsar, of the country of the
      'Sukhians[26]: silver, gold, pitchers of gold, tusks of
      the wild bull, staves, antimony, garments of many
      colors, and linen: I received.

   v The tribute of Garparunda, of the country of the Patin-
      ians: silver, gold, lead, bronze, gums, articles of
      bronze, tusks of wild bulls, and ebony[27]: I received.

[24] This is the Armenian *Muzri*, not Egypt.
[25] This would seem from the sculpture to mean a rhinoceros. Lenor-
mant, however, identifies it with the yak.
[26] Nomadic tribes in the southwest of Babylonia.
[27] The word means literally, "pieces of strong wood."

THE NIMROD INSCRIPTION OF TIGLATH-PILESER IV.

The palace of Tiglath-Pileser, the great King, the mighty King, King of the whole world, King of Assyria, King of Babylon, King of Sumer and Akkad, King of the four regions,

the mighty one, the warrior, who with the help of . . . like a flood overspread them, and as smoke reckoned them —

the King who at the command of Ashur, Shamash, and Marduk the great gods . . . from the sea [1] of Bit-Yakin to Bikni of the rising of the sun,

and the sea of the setting of the sun to Mutsri,[2] from the west to the east the countries ruled, and exercised kingship over them.

5 From the beginning of my kingship to seventeen years of my reign. The peoples of Itu'a, Rubu'a, Khamarani, Lukhuatu, Kharibu, Rubbu, Rapiqu, Khiranu, Rabilu,

Natsiru, Gulusu, Nabatu, Rakhiqu, Ka . . ., Rummulutu, Adilie, Kiprie, Ubudu, Gurumu, Bagdadu, Khindiru,

Damunu, Dunanu, Nilqu, Radie Da . . ., Ubulu, Karma', Ambatu, Ru'a, Qabi'a, Li'tau, Marusu,

Amatu, Khagaranu, the cities of Dur-Kurigalzi, Adi . . ., Birtu of Sarragiti, Birtu of Labbanat, Birtu of Kar-bel-matati,

the Arumu,[3] all of them, who are on the banks of the rivers Tigris, Euphrates, and 'Surappi, to the midst of the river Uknie, which is over against the lower

[1] Literally, "the bitter river," at the head of the Persian Gulf.
[2] Egypt.
[3] The Aramæans.

sea, I subdued, with slaughter of them I slaughtered, their spoil I spoiled.

10 The Arumu, as many as there were, to the territory of Assyria I added them, and my generals as governors over them I set.   Upon Tul-Kamri, which they call the city Khumut,

a city I built; Kar-ashur its name I called; people of the countries, the spoil of my hands, in the midst I placed.   In Sippara, Niffer, Babylon, Borsippa, Kutha, Kish, Dilbat, and Urbuk, cities without equals,

splendid sacrifices to Bel, Zirbanit, Nabu, Tasmit, Nergal, Laz, the great gods, my lords, I offered, and they loved my priesthood.   Broad Kar-Duniash [4] to its whole extent I ruled, and

exercised kingship over it.   The Puqudu [5] as it were with a net I struck down, with slaughter of them I slaughtered, much spoil of them I spoiled.   These Puqudu and the city of Lakhiru, which looks toward the midst of the city of Khilimmu,

and the city of Pillutu, which is on the side of Elam, to the territory of Assyria I added, and in the hands of my general, the governor of Arrapkha I allotted. The Kaldudu, as many as there were, I carried away, and

15 in the midst of Assyria I settled.   Kaldu [6] to its whole extent like dust I trod it down.   Nabuusabsi, son of Silani, his warriors, close to 'Sarrapanu, his city I slew,

and himself in front of the great gate of his city on a stake I lifted up, and I reduced his country to subjection.   'Sarrapanu by means of a wall and battering-engines I captured.   55,000 people, together with their goods,

his spoil, his stuff, his possessions, his wife, his sons, his

4 Babylonia.
5 The Pekod of Jer. l. 21.
6 The Chaldeans of classical antiquity, Sumer.

daughters, and his gods, I carried off. That city, together with the cities which are in its neighborhood, I destroyed, I laid waste, with fire I burned, and to mounds and ruins I reduced.

The city of Tarbatsu and city of Yapallu I captured. 30,000 people, together with their goods, their stuff, their possessions, and their gods, I carried off. Those cities, together with the cities which are in their neighborhood

like a ruin of the deluge I destroyed. Zaqiru, son of Sa'alli, against the ordinances of the great gods sinned, and with . . . his mouth. Him together with his great men with my hands I seized;

20 bonds of iron I put upon them, and to Assyria I took them. The people of Bit-Sa'alli were afraid, and the city of Dur . . . for their stronghold they took.

That city by siege and storm I took, and as earth [7] I reckoned. 50,400 people, together with their goods, their spoil, their stuff, their possessions, his wife, his sons, his daughters, and his gods, I carried off.

The city of Amlilatu I captured. The people, together with their goods, its spoil, its stuff, its possessions, I carried off. Bit-Sa'alli to its whole extent like a deluge I overspread, and I laid waste its homesteads.

Those countries to the territory of Assyria I added Ukinzir,[8] son of Amukkan, in 'Sapie, the city of his kingship, I besieged him; his fighting men in numbers in front of his great gate I slew.

The groves of palms, which were outside his wall, I cut down, and I did not leave one. His date-palms, which are the growth of the country, I destroyed, and his enclosures I broke down, and filled up the interiors. All his cities

25 I destroyed, I laid waste, with fire I burned. Bit-Silani, Bit-Amukkani, and Bit-Sa'alli to their whole extent

[7] Or, literally, "on the earth"; that is, "I threw to the ground," "leveled with the ground."

[8] The Khinziros of the Greek writers.

like a ruin of the deluge I destroyed; to mounds and ruins I reduced.

The tribute of Balasu,[9] son of Dakkuri, and of Nadin of Larak, silver, gold, precious stones I received. Mardukbaladan, son of Yakin, king of the sea,[10] who in the time of the kings, my fathers, into the presence of none of them had come, and

kissed their feet, fear of the Majesty of Ashur my lord cast him down, and to Sapia, into my presence, he came, and kissed my feet. Gold, the dust of his country, in abundance.

implements of gold, necklaces of gold, precious stones, the produce of the sea, beams of wood . . . particolored garments, perfumes in abundance of all kinds, oxen, sheep, as his tribute I received.

The countries of Namri, Bit-'Sangibuti, Bit-Khamban, 'Sumurzu, Barrua, Bit-Zualzas, Bit-Matti, the city of Niqu, which is in the country of Umliyas, the countries of Bit-Taranzai, Par'sua, Bit-Zatti,

30 Bit-Abadani, Bit-Kap'si, Bit-Sangi, Bit-Urzakki, Bit-Ishtar, the city of Zakruti,[11] the countries of Gizinikissi, Nissa,[12] the cities of Tsibur, Urimzan, the countries of Ra'usan,

. . . Niparia, Buztuz, Ariarmi, Burrumu-sarrani-itstsuru, 'Sak'sukni, Araquttu, Karzipra, Gukinnana, Bit-'Sakbat, Silkhazi,

which men called the stronghold of the Babylonian, Ruadi, Bit-Dur, Usqaqqana, Sikra the land of gold, districts of remote Media, to their whole extent like dust I overwhelmed, and

their fighting men in numbers I slew. 60,500 people, together with their goods, their horses, their mules, their humped oxen, their oxen, their sheep, without number, I carried off.

[9] This name corresponds to the classical Belesys.
[10] The country at the head of the Persian Gulf.
[11] The Asagartiya of the Persian cuneiform texts, the Sagartians of classical geography in the Zagros mountains.
[12] The Nisæa of classical geography.

Their cities I destroyed, I laid waste, and with fire I burned; to mounds and ruins I reduced.   The countries of Namri, Bit-'Sangibuti, Bit-Khamban, 'Sumurzu, Bit-Barrua, Bit-Zualzas,

35 Bit-Matti, Niqqu, which is in Umliyas, Bit-Taranzai, Par'sua, Bit-Zatti, Bit-Abdadani, Bit-Kap'si, Bit-'Sangi, Bit-Urzakki, the cities of Bit-Ishtar,

and Zakruti of remote Media, to the territory of Assyria I added.   The cities which were in them anew I built; the worship of Ashur my lord in the midst I established; people from the countries the conquests of my hands therein I settled;

my generals as governors over them I appointed; an image of my kingship in Tikrakki, the cities of Bit-Ishtar and Tsibur, the countries of Ariarmi, Barru-mu-sarrani-itstsuru,

'Silkhazi, which men called the stronghold of the Babylonian, I set up.   The tribute of Media and Ellipai,[13] and the chiefs of the cities of the mountains, all of them, as far as Bikni,

horses, mules, humped oxen, oxen, and sheep . . . the might and majesty of Ashur my lord, which in the mountains, all of them . . .

40 . . . of Ashur my lord cast him down, and to Dur-Tiglath-Pileser, the city which . . . into my presence he came, and kissed my feet.

   . . . mules, oxen, and sheep, weapons . . .

   . . . my general Ashurdaninani to the land of the mighty Medes, the land of the rising sun . . .

   . . . the land of Kirkhu in its totality I captured; to the territory of Assyria I added . . .

   . . . of my kingship therein I placed; the worship of Ashur my lord therein I established . . .

45 . . . the people of Ararat 'Sulumal of the country of the Meliddians,[14] Tarkhu-lara of the Gangumians . . .

---

[13] Ellip was the district of which Ekbatana was subsequently the capital.

[14] Melid, the modern Malatiyeh in eastern Kappadokia.

... Kustaspi, of the country of the Komagenians, to capture and plunder ...

... the countries of Kistan and Khalpi districts of ...

... *assunu* the river Sinzi, the canal like *nabasi* ...

... I seized them in the midst of ...

50 ... royal beds ...

. . . .

... which into my presence ...

... the cities of the Temanians,[15] the Sabæans,[16] the Khaiappians, the Bananians ...

... whom no one knows, and whose seat is distant, the Majesty of my Lordship ...

55 ... camels, she-camels, perfumes in abundance of all kinds, as their tribute like one to ...

Idibi'ili as a watch over against Egypt I appointed. In the countries all of them, which ...

The tribute of Kustaspi of the Komagenians, Urik of the Quans,[17] Sibittibi'il of Gebal ...

Enilu of Hamath, Panammu of the 'Sam'lians,[18] Tarkhulara of the Gamgumians, 'Sulumal of the Meliddians ...

Uas-surme of Tubal, Uskhitti of the Tunians, Urpalla of the Tukhanians, Tukhamme of the Istundians ...

60 Matanbi'il of Arvad, 'Sanipu of Bit-Ammon, 'Salamanu (Solomon) of the Moabites ...

Mitinti of Ashkelon, Jehoahaz of Judah, Quasmelech of Edom, Muz ...

Hanon of Gaza, gold, silver, lead, iron, *abar,* parti-colored clothing, garments, the dress of their country, purple ...

... the produce of sea and land, the spoil of their country, the treasure of royalty, horses, mules, the team of a yoke ...

---

[15] The Teman of the Old Testament.

[16] 'Sab'ai, the Sheba of the Old Testament.

[17] On the northern shore of the Gulf of Antioch.

[18] 'Samahla lay to the northeast of the Gulf of Antioch, its capital being now represented by the mounds of Sinjirli.

Uas-surme of Tabal, the things of Assyria sought to rival,
and into my presence did not come; my general the
Rabsak . . .

65 Khulli, the son of an unknown person, [19] on the throne of
his royalty I seated.   10 talents of gold, 1,000 talents of silver, 2000 horses . . .

my general, the Rab-shakeh, to Tyre I sent.   Of Mie-
tenna of Tyre 150 talents of gold . . .

with the sense, the cunning, the penetrating thought,
which the chief of the gods, the prince Nudimmut [20]
gave me, a palace of cedar . . .

and an entrance-hall after the fashion of a palace of the
Hittites for my majesty in Calah I built . . .

An amount of earth higher than the former palaces of my
fathers from the bed of the Tigris I caused to
raise . . .

70 All the men of my army, such as were cunning, skilfully
I employed, and . . .

20 great cubits below the rushing [21] water stout, squared
stone like the mass of a mountain I piled, and
left . . .

their terraces I laid out, and their foundations I fixed,
and I raised their spires.   Half a *gar,* two-thirds of
a cubit the house . . . I devised, and . . .

On the north side in front I placed their gates, with ivory,
usu-wood,   box-wood,   palm-wood,   box-wood . . .
juniper.

The tribute of the kings of the Hittites, the princes of
Aram and Kaldi, whom by the pre-eminence of my
strength I had subdued to my feet . . . I stored
therein.

75 5½ *gar,* four cubits sheer from the depth of the water
their fabric I enclosed, and more than the palaces of
all lands I enlarged . . . their work.

With beams of cedar, well grown, which like the fra-

[19] Literally, " the son of no one."
[20] The god Ea.
[21] Literally, " strong "; *i.e.,* " strong-flowing."

grance of the wood of Khasurri [22] for their perfume are good, the produce of Khamana,[23] Lebanon and Ammanana,

I roofed them, and made them fast.   To show forth ornament . . . stones, the work of *burkulluti,* I made, and therewith I furnished the gate.

Doors of cedar and cypress, in pairs, the entering in of which is blissful, whose fragrance breathes upon the heart,

with a rim of bronze and shining metal I bound, and in the gates I fixed.   Lions, bulls, winged bulls, formed with exceeding cunning, skilfully fashioned,

80 the entrances I caused to hold, and for wonderment I set up; thresholds looking toward the sun, of *paruti*-stone, at their base I laid down, and I made glorious the entrance.

An image, too, I made to keep guard over the great gods; with creatures of sea and land I surrounded him; with terror I invested him.

With a railing of gold, silver, and copper for their completion I surrounded them, and I made their forms to shine.

For the dwelling of my royalty its buildings I raised; precious stones, the work . . . I placed within it.

The palaces — "Pleasure," "Holding abundance," "King's graciousness," "Making their builder grow old," for their names I called.

85 The gates —"Righteousness," "Ordering the judgment of the princes of the four regions," "Preserving the tribute of mountains and seas,"

"Causing the fulness of the lands to enter into the presence of the King their lord," I named the names of their gates.

[22] Khasur was the name of one of the spurs of Mount Amanus.
[23] Amanus at the head of the Gulf of Antioch.

THE INSCRIPTION OF SARGON II.

(IN HIS PALACE AT KHORSABAD)

Palace of Sargon, the great King, the powerful King, King of the legions, King of Assyria, Viceroy of the gods at Babylon, King of the Sumers and of the Akkads, favorite of the great gods.

The gods Ashur, Nebu, and Marduk have conferred on me the royalty of the nations, and they have propagated the memory of my fortunate name to the ends of the earth. I have followed the reformed precepts of Sippara, Nippur, Babylon, and Borsippa; I have amended the imperfections which the men of all laws had admitted.

I have reunited the dominions of Kalu, Ur, Orchoe, Erikhi, Larsa, Kullab, Kisik, the dwelling-place of the god Laguda; I have subdued their inhabitants. As to the laws of Sumer and of the town of Harran, which had fallen into desuetude from the most ancient times, I have restored to fresh vigor their forgotten customs.

The great gods have made me happy by the constancy of their affection, they have granted me the exercise of my sovereignty over all kings; they have reestablished obedience upon them all. From the day of my accession there existed no princes who were my masters; I have not, in combats or battles, seen my victor. I have crushed the territories of the rebels like straws, and I have struck them with the plagues of the four elements. I have opened innumerable deep and very extensive forests, I have leveled their inequalities. I have traversed winding and thick valleys, which were impenetrable, like a needle, and I passed in digging tanks dug on my way.

5 By the grace and power of the great gods, my Masters, I have flung my arms; by my force I have defeated my ene-

mies. I have ruled from Iatnan,[1] which is in the middle of the sea of the setting sun, to the frontiers of Egypt and of the country of the Moschians, over vast Phenicia, the whole of Syria, the whole of *guti muski* of distant Media, near the country of Bikni, to the country of Ellip, from Ras, which borders upon Elam, to the banks of the Tigris, to the tribes of Itu, Rubu, Haril, Kaldud, Hauran, Ubul, Ruhua, of the Litai who dwells on the borders of the Surappi and the Ukne, Gambul, Khindar, and Pukud.[2] I have reigned over the *suti* hunters who are in the territory of Iatbur, in whatever it was as far as the towns of Samhun, Bab-Dur, Dur-Tilit, Khilikh, Pillat, Dunni-Samas, Bubi, Tel-Khumba, which are in the dependency of Elam,[3] and Kar-duniash[4] Upper and Lower, of the countries of Bit-Amukkan, Bit-Dakkur, Bit-Silan, Bit-Sa'alla, which together form Chaldea in its totality, over the country of Bit-Iakin, which is on the sea-shore, as far as the frontier of Dilmun. I have received their tributes, I have established my lieutenants over them as governors, and I have reduced them under my suzerainty.

This is what I did from the beginning of my reign to my fifteenth year of reign:

I defeated Khumbanigas, King of Elam, in the plains of Kalu.

I besieged and occupied the town of Samaria, and took 27,280 of its inhabitants captive. I took from them 50 chariots, but left them the rest of their belongings. I placed my lieutenants over them; I renewed the obligation imposed upon them by one of the Kings who preceded me.

Hanun, King of Gaza, and Sebech, Sultan[5] of Egypt, allied

[1] Itanus, or Yatnan, in the island of Crete, became afterward the name of the island of Cyprus.
[2] The Pekod of the Bible (Jer. i. 21; Ezek. xxiii. 23).
[3] Which belongs to Elam.
[4] Nearly all the names of the Elamite towns are Semitic (see Gen. x. 22), but the Susian ones are not.
[5] This is the word *siltan*, the Hebrew *shilton* ("power"), the Arabic *sultan*.

themselves at Rapih [6] to oppose me, and fight against me; they came before me, I put them to flight. Sebech yielded before my cohorts, he fled, and no one has ever seen any trace of him since. I took with my own hand Hanun, King of Gaza.

I imposed a tribute on Pharaoh, King of Egypt; Samsie, Queen of Arabia; It-amar, the Sabean, of gold, sweet smelling herbs of the land, horses, and camels.

10 Kiakku of Sinukhta had despised the god Ashur, and refused submission to him. I took him prisoner, and seized his 30 chariots and 7,350 of his soldiers. I gave Sinuhta, the town of his royalty, to Matti from the country of Tuna, I added some horses and asses to the former tribute, and appointed Matti as governor.

Amris of Tabal had been placed upon the throne of Khulli his father; I gave to him a daughter and I gave him Cilicia,[7] which had never submitted to his ancestors. But he did not keep the treaty and sent his ambassador to Urzaha, King of Armenia, and to Mita, King of the Moschians, who had seized my provinces. I transported Amris to Assyria, with his belongings, the members of his ancestors' families, and the magnates of the country, as well as 100 chariots; I established some Assyrians, devoted to my government, in their places. I appointed my lieutenant-governor over them, and commanded tributes to be levied upon them.

Jaubid of Hamath, a smith,[8] was not the legitimate master of the throne; he was an infidel and an impious man, and he had coveted the royalty of Hamath. He incited the towns of Arpad, Simyra, Damascus, and Samaria to rise against me, took his precautions with each of them, and prepared for battle. I counted all the troops of the god Ashur; in the town of Karkar, which had declared itself for the rebel, I besieged him and his warriors, I occupied

[6] Raphia, near the frontier of Egypt.

[7] Khilakku. It seems to be identical with the Sparda of Persian, the Sepharad of Obadiah.

[8] The condition of Jaubid before his accession.

Karkar and reduced it to ashes. I took him, himself, and had him flayed, and I killed the chief of the rioters in each town, and reduced them to a heap of ruins. I recruited my forces with 200 chariots and 600 horsemen from among the inhabitants of the country of Hamath and added them to my empire.

Whilst Iranzu, of Van, lived, he was subservient and devoted to my rule, but fate removed him. His subjects placed his son Aza on the throne. Urzaha, the Armenian, intrigued with the people of Mount Mildis, Zikirta, Misiandi, with the nobles of Van, and enticed them to rebellion; they threw the body of their Master Aza on the top of the mountains. Ullusun, of Van, his brother, whom they had placed on his father's throne, did homage to Urzaha, and gave him 22 fortresses with their garrisons. In the anger of my heart I counted all the armies of the god Ashur, I watched like a lion in ambush and advanced to attack these countries. Ullusun, of Van, saw my expedition approaching; he set out with his troops and took up a strong position in the ravines of the high mountains. I occupied Izirti, the town of his royalty, and the towns of Izibia and Armit, his formidable fortresses, I reduced them to ashes. I killed all that belonged to Urzaha, the Armenian, in these high mountains. I took with my own hand 250 royal members of his family. I occupied 55 royal towns, of which 8 were ordinary towns and 11 impregnable fortresses. I reduced them to ashes. I incorporated the 22 strong towns, that Ullusun of Van had delivered to him with Assyria. I occupied 8 strong cities of the country of Tuaya and the districts of Tilusina of Andia; 4,200 men, with their belongings, were carried away into slavery.

Mitatti, of Zikirta, had secured himself against my arms; he and the men of his country had fled into the forests; no trace of them was to be seen. I reduced Parda, the town of his royalty, to ashes; I occupied 23 great towns in the environs, and I spoiled them. The cities of Suandakhul and Zurzukka, of the country of Van, took the part of

Mitatti; I occupied and pillaged them. Then I took Bagadatti of the Mount Mildis, and I had him flayed. I banished Dayaukku and his suite to Hamath, and I made them dwell there.

15 Then Ullusun heard in his high mountains of my glorious exploits: he departed in haste like a bird, and kissed my feet; I pardoned his innumerable misdeeds, and I blotted out his iniquities. I granted pardon to him; I replaced him upon the throne of his royalty. I gave him the two fortresses and the 22 great towns that I had taken away from Urzaha and Mitatti. I endeavored to restore peace to his country. I made the image of my Majesty: I wrote on it the glory of the god Ashur, my Master, I erected many fac-similes of it in Izirti, the town of his royalty.

I imposed a tribute of horses, oxen, and lambs upon Ianzu, King of the river country, in Hupuskia, the town of his power.

Ashurlih, of Kar-Alla, Itti, of Allapur, had sinned against Ashur and despised his power. I had Ashurlih flayed. I banished the men of Kar-Alla, whoever they were, and Itti, with his suite, I placed them in Hamath.

I took the inhabitants of the towns of Sukkia, Bala, Ahitikna, Pappa, Lallukni, away from their homes; I made them dwell at Damascus in Syria.

I occupied the 6 towns of the country of Niksamma, I took with my own hand Nirisar, governor of the town of Surgadia; I added these towns to the satrapy of Parsuas.

20 Bel-sar-usur[9] was King of the town of Kisisim; I had him transported to Assyria with all that he possessed, his treasure, the contents of his palace; I put my lieutenant in as governor of the town, to which I gave the name of Kar-Marduk. I had an image made of my Majesty and erected it in the middle of the town. I occupied 6 towns in the neighborhood and I added them to his government.

I attacked and conquered Kibaba, prefect of the town of Kharkhar, I took him and the inhabitants of his country

[9] The same name as Belshazzar.

captive, I rebuilt this city and made the inhabitants of the provinces, that my arm had conquered, live there. I placed my lieutenant as governor over them. I named the town Kar-Sarkin; I established the worship of the god Ashur, my Master, there. I erected an image of my Royal self. I occupied 6 towns in the environs, and added them to his government.

I besieged and took the towns of Tel-Akhi-tub, Khindau, Bagai, and Anzaria; I transported the inhabitants of them to Assyria. I rebuilt them; I gave them the names of Kar-Nabu, Kar-Sin, Kar-Ben, Kar-Ishtar.

To maintain my position in Media, I have erected fortifications in the neighborhood of Kar-Sarkin. I occupied 34 towns in Media and annexed them to Assyria, and I levied annual tributes of horses upon them.

I besieged and took the town of Eristana, and the surrounding towns in the country of Bait-Ili; I carried away the spoil.

25 The countries of Agag and Ambanda,[10] in Media, opposite the Arabs of the East, had refused their tributes; I destroyed them, laid them waste, and burnt them by fire.

Dalta, of Ellip, was subject to me, and devoted to the worship of Ashur; 5 of his towns revolted and no longer recognized his dominion. I came to his aid, I besieged and occupied these towns, I carried the men and their goods with numberless horses away into Assyria.

Urzana, of the town of Musasir, had attached himself to Urzaha, the Armenian, and had refused me his allegiance. With the multitude of my army, I covered the city of Musasir as if it were with ravens, and he to save his life fled alone into the mountains.

I entered as a ruler into Musasir. I seized as spoil Urzana's wife, sons and daughters, his money, his treasures, all the stores of his palace whatever they were, with 20,100 men and all that they possessed, the gods Haldia and Bagabarta, his gods, and their holy vessels in great numbers.

[10] Ambanda is perhaps the Median " Kampanda."

Urzaha, King of Armenia, heard of the defeat of Musasir and the carrying away of the god Haldia[11] his god; he cut off his life by his own hands with a dagger of his girdle. I held a severe judgment over the whole of Armenia. I spread over the men who inhabit this country mourning and lamentation.

30 Tarhunazi, of the town of Melid, sought for revenge. He sinned against the laws of the great gods, and refused his submission. In the anger of my heart, I crushed like briars Melid, which was the town of his kingdom, and the neighboring towns. I made him, his wife, sons and daughters, the slaves of his palace whoever they were, with 5,000 warriors, leave Tel-Garimmi; I treated them all as booty. I rebuilt Tel-Garimmi; I had it entirely occupied by some archers from the country of Khammanua, which my hand had conquered, and I added it to the boundaries of this country. I put it in the hands of my lieutenant, and I restituted the surface of the dominion, as it had been in the time of Gunzinan, the preceding King.

Tarhular, of Gamgum, had a son Muttallu, who had murdered his father by the arms, and sat on the throne against my will, and to whom they had entrusted their country. In the anger of my heart, I hastily marched against the town of Markasi, with my chariots and horsemen, who followed on my steps. I treated Muttallu, his son and the families of the country of Bit-Pa'alla in its totality, as captives, and seized as booty the gold and silver and the numberless treasures of his palace. I reinstated the men of Gamgum and the neighboring tribes, and placed my lieutenant as governor over them; I treated them like the Assyrians.

Azuri, King of Ashdod,[12] determined within himself to render no more tributes; he sent hostile messages against Assyria to the neighboring kings. I meditated ven-

[11] We find in the inscriptions of Van the god Haldi as god of the Armenians.

[12] See Isaiah xx. 1.

geance for this, and I withdrew from him the government over his country. I put his brother Akhimit on his throne. But the people of Syria, eager for revolt, got tired of Akhimit's rule, and installed Iaman, who, like the former, was not the legitimate master of the throne. In the anger of my heart, I did not assemble the bulk of my army nor divide my baggage, but I marched against Ashdod with my warriors, who did not leave the trace of my feet.

Iaman learned from afar of the approach of my expedition; he fled beyond Egypt toward Libya (Meluhhi),[13] and no one ever saw any further trace of him. I besieged and took Ashdod and the town of Gimtu-Asdudim;[14] I carried away captive Iaman's gods, his wife, his sons, his daughters, his money, and the contents of his palace, together with the inhabitants of his country. I built these towns anew and placed in them the men that my arm had conquered.

I placed my lieutenant as governor over them, and I treated them as Assyrians. They never again became guilty of impiety.

35 The King of Libya lives in the middle of the desert, in an inaccessible place, at a month's journey. From the most remote times until the renewal of the lunar period his fathers had sent no ambassadors to the kings, my ancestors, to ask for peace and friendship and to acknowledge the power of Marduk. But the immense terror inspired by my Majesty roused him, and fear changed his intentions. In fetters of iron he threw him (Iaman), directed his steps toward Assyria and kissed my feet.

Muttallu, of Commagene, a fraudulent and hostile man, did not honor the memory of the gods, he plotted a conspiracy, and meditated defection. He trusted upon Argisti, King of Armenia, a helper who did not assist him, took upon himself the collection of the tributes and his

---

[13] Meluhhi is not Meroe, but Libya, and especially the Marmarica. The name seems to be the Milyes of Herodotus.

[14] *Asdudim* seems to be a Hebraic plural.

part of the spoil, and refused me his submission. In the anger of my heart, I took the road to his country with the chariots of my power, and the horsemen who never left the traces of my feet. Muttallu saw the approach of my expedition, he withdrew his troops, and no one saw any further trace of him. I besieged and occupied his capital and 62 large towns all together. I carried away his wife, his sons, his daughters, his money, his treasure, all precious things from his palace, together with the inhabitants of his country as spoil, I left none of them. I inaugurated this town afresh; I placed in it men from the country of Bit-Iakin, that my arm had conquered. I instituted my lieutenant as governor, and subdued them under my rule. I previously took from them 150 chariots, 1,500 horsemen, 20,000 archers, 1,000 men armed with shields and lances, and I confided the country to my satrap.

While Dalta, King of Ellip, lived, he was submissive and devoted to my rule; the infirmities of age, however, came and he walked on the path of death. Nibie and Ispabara, the sons of his wives, claimed the vacant throne of his royalty, the country and the taxes, and they fought a battle. Nibie applied to Sutruk-Nakhunti, King of Elam, to support his claims, giving to him pledges for his alliance, and the other came as a helper. Ispabara, on his side, implored me to maintain his cause, and to encourage him, at the same time bowing down, and humbling himself, and asking my alliance. I sent seven of my lieutenants with their armies to support his claims; they put Nibie and the army of the four rivers, which had helped him to flight, at the town of Mareobisti. I reinstated Ispabara on the throne; I reestablished peace in his country, and confided it to his care.

Marduk-Baladan, son of Iakin, King of Chaldea, the fallacious, the persistent in enmity, did not respect the memory of the gods; he trusted in the sea, and in the retreat of the marshes; he eluded the precepts of the great gods, and refused to send his tributes. He had supported as

an ally Khumbanigas, King of Elam. He had excited all
the nomadic tribes of the desert against me. He prepared himself for battle, and advanced. During twelve
years,[15] against the will of the gods of Babylon, the town
of Bel, which judges the gods, he had excited the country
of the Sumers and Akkads, and had sent ambassadors to
them. In honor of the god Ashur, the father of the gods,
and of the great and august Lord Marduk, I roused my
courage, I prepared my ranks for battle. I decreed an
expedition against the Chaldeans, an impious and riotous
people. Marduk-Baladan heard of the approach of my
expedition, dreading the terror of his own warriors, he
fled before it, and flew in the night-time like an owl, fall-
ing back from Babylon, to the town of Ikbibel. He assembled together the towns possessing oracles, and the
gods living in these towns he brought to save them to Dur-
Iakin, fortifying its walls. He summoned the tribes of
Gambul, Pukud, Tamun, Ruhua, and Khindar, put them
in this place, and prepared for battle. He calculated the
extent of a plethrum in front of the great wall. He con-
structed a ditch 200 spans wide, and deep one fathom and
a half. The conduits of water, coming from the Euphrates, flowed out into this ditch; he had cut off the
course of the river, and divided it into canals, he had
surrounded the town, the place of his revolt, with a dam,
he had filled it with water and cut off the conduits. Marduk-Baladan, with his allies and his soldiers, had the
insignia of his royalty kept as in an island on the banks
of the river; he arranged his plan of battle. I stretched
my combatants all along the river, dividing them into
bands; they conquered the enemies. By the blood of the
rebels the waters of these canals reddened like dyed wool.
The nomadic tribes were terrified by this disaster which
surprised him, and fled; I completely separated his allies
and the men of Marsan from him; I filled the ranks of
the insurgents with mortal terror. He left in his tent
the insignia of his royalty, the golden . . ., the golden

[15] From 721 to 709 B.C.

throne, the golden parasol, the golden scepter, the silver chariot, the golden ornaments, and other effects of considerable weight; he fled alone, and disappeared like the ruined battlements of his fortress, and I entered into his retreat. I besieged and occupied the town of Dur-Iakin; I took as spoil and made captive, him, his wife, his sons, his daughters, the gold and silver and all that he possessed, the contents of his palace, whatever it was, with considerable booty from the town. I made each family, and every man who had withdrawn himself from my arms, accountable for this sin. I reduced Dur-Iakin, the town of his power, to ashes. I undermined and destroyed its ancient forts. I dug up the foundation-stone; I made it like a thunder-stricken ruin. I allowed the people of Sippara, Nipud, Babylon, and Borsippa, who live in the middle of the towns, to exercise their profession, to enjoy their belongings in peace, and I have watched upon them. I took away the possession of the fields, which from remote times had been in the hand of the *Suti* Nomad, and restored them to their rightful owners. I placed the nomadic tribes of the desert again under my yoke, and I restored the forgotten land delimitations which had existed during the tranquillity of the land. I gave to each of the towns of Ur, Orchoe, Erikhi, Larsa, Kullab, and Kisik, the dwelling of the god Laguda, the god that resides in each, and I restored the gods, who had been taken away, to their sanctuaries. I reestablished the altered laws in full force.

I imposed tributes on the countries of Bet-Iakin, the high and low part, and on the towns of Samhun, Bab-Dur, Dur-Tilit, Bubi, Tel-Khumba, which are the resort of Elam. I transplanted into Elam the inhabitants of the Commagene, in Syria, that I had attacked with my own hand, obeying the commands of the great gods my Masters, and I placed them on the territory of Elam, in the town of Sakbat. Nabu-Pakid-Ilan was authorized to collect the taxes from the Elamites in order to govern them; I claimed as a pledge the town of Birtu. I placed all this

country in the hands of my lieutenant at Babylon and my
lieutenant in the country of Gambul.

40 I returned alone to Babylon, to the sanctuaries of Bel, the
judge of the gods, in the excitement of my heart and the
splendor of my appearance; I took the hands of the great
Lord, the august god Marduk, and I traversed the way to
the chamber of the spoil.

I transported into it 154 talents 26 minas 10 drachms of
gold *russu*,[16] 1804 talents 20 minas of silver,[17] ivory, a
great deal of copper, iron in an innumerable quantity,
some of the stone *ka,* alabaster, the minerals *pi digili,*
flattened *pi sirru* for witness seals, blue and purple stuffs,
cloth of *berom* and cotton, ebony; cedar, and cypress
wood, freshly cut from the fine forests on Mount Amanus,
in honor of Bel, Zarpanit, Nabu, and Tasmit, and the gods
who inhabit the sanctuaries of the Sumers, and Akkads;
all that from my accession to the third year of my reign.[18]

Upir, King of Dilmun, who dwells at the distance of 30 para-
sangs [19] in the midst of the sea of the rising sun and who
is established as a fish, heard of the favor that the gods
Ashur, Nabu, and Marduk had accorded me; he sent
therefore his expiatory gift.

And the seven Kings of the country of Iahnagi, of the country
of Iatnan (who have established and extended their
dwellings at a distance of seven days' navigation in the
midst of the sea of the setting sun, and whose name from
the most ancient ages until the renewal of the lunar
period [20] none of the Kings, my fathers, in Assyria and
Chaldea had heard), had been told of my lofty achieve-
ments in Chaldea and Syria, and my glory, which had

16 12,544, pd. troy, 68.

17 152,227, pd. troy, 75. A royal silver drachm is about seventy
cents, a royal mina nearly $44; the State drachm and mina is the half
of it. A silver talent is about $1300.

18 Sargon speaks of his third "year" and not of his third campaign,
in order to mark what he had already accomplished before the year 717.

19 One hundred and ten miles.

20 This is the second passage where Sargon alludes to this period end-
ing under his reign.

spread from afar to the midst of the sea. They subdued their pride and humbled themselves; they presented themselves before me at Babylon, bearing metals, gold, silver, vases, ebony-wood, and the manufactures of their country; they kissed my feet.

While I endeavored to exterminate Bet-Iakin and reduce Aram, and render my rule more efficacious in the country of Iatbur, which is beyond Elam, my lieutenant, the governor of the country of Kue, attacked Mita, the Moschian, and 3,000 of his towns; he demolished these towns, destroyed them, burnt them with fire, and led away many captives. And this Mita, the Moschian, who had never submitted to the Kings, my predecessors, and had never changed his will, sent his envoy to me to the very borders of the sea of the rising sun, bearing professions of allegiance and tributes.

45 In these days, these nations and these countries that my hand has conquered, and that the gods Ashur, Nabu, and Marduk have made bow to my feet, followed the ways of piety. With their help I built at the feet of the *musri* following the divine will and the wish of my heart, a town that I called *Dur-Sarkin* [21] to replace Nineveh.[22] Nisroch, Sin, Shamash, Nabu, Bin, Ninip, and their great spouses, who procreate eternally in the lofty temple of the upper and the nether world (Aralli) blessed the splendid wonders, the superb streets in the town of Dur-Sarkin. I reformed the institutions which were not agreeable to their ideas. The priests, the *nisi ramki*, the *surmahhi supar*, disputed at their learned discussions about the pre-eminence of their divinities, and the efficacy of their sacrifices.

[21] Or " Dur-Sarkayan." The King passes rapidly over some other peculiarities which he inserts in other texts, namely, the measures of the town, and the ceremonies of its edification. The circuit is given as containing 3 1-3 *ners* (miles) 1 stadium 3 canes 2 spans, or 24,740 spans, and Botta's measurings afford 6,790 metres (7,427 yds.). This statement gives for the span, with a slight correction in the fourth decimal, 27,425 cm. (10.797 ins., and for the cubit 5,485 cm. 21.594 ins.).

[22] At this time the palace of Nineveh was still in ruins. It was rebuilt by Sennacherib.

I built in the town some palaces covered with the skin of
the sea-calf, and of sandalwood, ebony, the wood of mastic tree, cedar, cypress, wild pistachio-nut tree, a palace of
incomparable splendor, as the seat of my royalty. I
placed their *dunu* upon tablets of gold, silver, alabaster,
tilpe stones, *parut* stones, copper, lead, iron, tin, and
khibisti made of earth. I wrote thereupon the glory of
the gods. Above I built a platform of cedar-beams. I
bordered the doors of pine and mastic wood with bronze
garnitures, and I calculated their distance. I made a
spiral staircase similar to the one in the great temple of
Syria, that is called in the Phenician language, *Bethil-
anni.* Between the doors I placed 8 double lions whose
weight is 1 *ner* 6 *soss,* 50 talents of first-rate copper, made
in honor of Mylitta . . . and their four *kubur* in mate-
rials from Mount Amanus; I placed them on *nirgalli.*
Over them I sculptured artistically a crown of a beast of
the fields, a bird in stone of the mountains. Toward the
four celestial regions I turned their front. The lintels
and the uprights I made in large gypsum stone that I
had taken away with my own hand, I placed them above.
I walled them in and I drew upon me the admiration of
the people of the countries.

From the beginning to the end I walked, worshiping the
god Ashur, and, following the custom of wise men, I built
palaces, I amassed treasures.

In the month of blessing, on the happy day, I invoked, in
the midst of them, Ashur, the father of the gods, the
greatest sovereign of the gods and the Istarat,[23] who inhabit Assyria. I presented vessels of glass, things in
chased silver, ivory, valuable jewels and immense presents, in great quantities, and I rejoiced their heart. I
exhibited sculptured idols, double and winged, some
. . . winged, some . . . winged, serpents, fishes, and
birds, from unknown regions and abysses, the . . .[24] in

[23] The Hebrew " Astaroth," which signifies " goddesses." (Compare
Judges x. 6.)
[24] Obscure.

high mountains, summits of the lands that I have conquered with my own hand, for the glory of my royalty.
As a worshiper of the gods and the god Ashur, I sacri-
ficed in their presence, with the sacrifice of white lambs,
holy holocausts of expiation, in order to withdraw the
gifts that had not been agreeable to the gods.

He has granted me in his august power a happy existence,
long life, and I obtained a constantly lucky reign. I
have entrusted myself to his favor.

50 The great Lord Bel-El, the Master of the lands, inhabits
the lofty tracts; the gods and Istarat inhabit Assyria;
their legions remain there in *pargiti,* and *martakni.*

With the chiefs of provinces, the satraps, wise men, astrono-
mers, magnates, the lieutenants and governors of Assyria,
I have ruled in my palace, and administered justice.

I have bid them take gold, silver, gold and silver vessels,
precious stones, copper, iron, considerable products of
mountains the mines of which are rich, cloth of *berom*
and cotton, blue and purple cloth, amber, skins of sea-
calves, pearls, sandalwood, ebony, horses from higher
Egypt,[25] asses, mules, camels, oxen. With all these numerous tributes I have rejoiced the heart of the gods.

May Ashur, the father of the gods, bless these palaces, by
giving to his images a spontaneous splendor. May he
watch over the issue even to the remote future. May the
sculptured bull, the protector and god who imparts per-
fection, dwell in day and in night-time in his presence,
and never stir from this threshold!

With the help of Ashur, may the King who has built these
palaces attain an old age, and may his offspring multiply
greatly! May these battlements last to the most remote
future! May he who dwells there come forth surrounded
with the greatest splendor; may he rejoice in his cor-
poral health, in the satisfaction of his heart accomplish
his wishes, attain his end, and may he render his mag-
nificence seven times more imposing!

25 It is not clear what animals are meant.

THE INSCRIPTION OF SENNACHERIB

Sennacherib, the great King, the powerful King,
the King of the world, the King of Assyria, the King of
    the four zones,
the wise shepherd, the favorite of the great gods,
the protector of justice, the lover of righteousness,
5 he who gives help, who goes to assist the weak,
who frequents the sanctuaries, the perfect hero,
the manful warrior, the first of all princes,
the great, he who destroys the rebellious,
who destroys the enemies;
10 Ashur, the great rock, a kingdom without a rival
has granted me.
Over all who sit on sacred seats has he made my arms
    great,
from the upper sea of the setting sun,
unto the lower sea of the rising sun [1]
15 the whole of the black-headed people [2] has he thrown
    beneath my feet
and rebellious princes shunned battle with me.
They forsook their dwellings; like a falcon
which dwells in the clefts, they fled alone to an inacces-
    sible place.
In my first campaign I accomplished the destruction of
    Marduk-baladan
20 King of Kar-duniash,[3] together with the troops of Elam,
his allies, near Kish.
In the midst of that battle he left his encampment
and fled alone, and saved his life.
The chariots, horses, freight-wagons, and mules
25 which he left in the onset of battle, my hands seized.

[1] Lake Van and the Persian Gulf.
[2] The inhabitants of Babylonia.
[3] Babylonia.

Into his palace I entered joyously and
opened his treasure-house. Gold, silver,
gold and silver utensils, costly stones of every kind,
possessions and goods, without number, a heavy spoil,
    his women of the palace,
30 *valets de chambre,* youths and maidens,
all the artizans, as many as there were,
the portable things of his palace, I brought forth and
counted as spoil. By the power of Ashur my lord,
75 of his powerful cities, the fortresses of the land of
    Kaldi,
35 and 420 smaller cities of their environs
I besieged, captured, and carried off their spoil.
The Arabians, Aramæans, and Chaldeans of Uruk,
Nippur, Kish, Kharsak-kalamma, Kutu, and Sippara
together with the inhabitants of the city who had com-
    mitted transgression,
40 I brought forth and counted as spoil. On my return
    march,
the Tu'muna, the Rikhikhu, the Yadaqqu,
the Ubudu, the Kipre, the Malakhu,
the Gurumu, the Ubulum, the Damunu,
the Gambulum, the Khindaru, the Ru'ua,
45 the Puqudu, the Khamranu, the Khagaranu,
the Nabatu, the Li'tau, Aramæans
who were rebellious, I conquered together.
208,000 people, young and old, male and female,
7200 horses and mules, 11,073 asses, 5230 camels,
50 80,100 cattle, 800,600 sheep, an immense
spoil, I carried away to Assyria.
In the course of my campaign, I received from Nabu-
    bel-shanati,
the prefect of the city Khararati, gold, silver,
tall palms, asses, camels, cattle,
55 and sheep, a great present.
The men of the city Khirimme, a rebellious enemy,
I cast down with arms, I left not one alive,
their corpses I bound on stakes

and placed them round the city. That district
60 I took anew. 1 steer, 10 rams,
10 measures [4] of wine, 20 measures of dates, their first
    fruits,
for the gods of Assyria, my lords, I established forever.
In my second campaign, Ashur, my lord, gave me con-
    fidence.
Against the land of the Cossæans,[5] and the land of the
    Yasubigallai,
65 who in former times to the kings, my forefathers,
had not submitted, I marched. Over high, wooded
    mountains,
a rough country, I went on horseback.
I brought up the chariot of my feet, with ropes.
A steep place I climbed like a wild bull.
70 Bit-Kilamzakh, Khardishpi, Bit-Kubatti —
his cities, powerful fortresses, I besieged and captured.
Men, horses, mules, asses,
cattle, and sheep from them
I brought forth, and counted as spoil; but their small
    cities,
75 without number, I destroyed, wasted, and made like
    fields,
the tents, their dwelling-places, I burned with fire,
I reduced to ashes. I made that city Bit-Kilamzakh
into a fortress, stronger than before
I made its walls; the people of the countries,
80 the possession of my hands, I made to dwell therein.
The people of the land of the Cossæans, and of the land
    of Yasubigallai,
who had fled before my arms,

COLUMN II

from the mountains I made them descend,
in Khardishpi and Bit-Kubatti I made them settle;

---

[4] *Imeri,* *i.e.,* "donkey-loads," the original meaning of the word
homer.

[5] *Kasshi.* They lived in the mountains on the east of Babylonia.

in the hands of my deputy, the governor of Arrapkha,[6]
I placed them; a tablet I caused to be prepared;
5 the victory of my hands which
I had gained over them I wrote upon it and
I set it up in the city.   I turned about and
to the land of Ellipi [7] I took my way.
Before me Ispabara, their King, left his strong cities,
10 his treasure-houses, and fled
   away.   The whole of his extensive land I wasted like
      a storm-wind.
Marubishti and Akuddu, cities
of his royal house, together with 34 small cities of their
      environs,
I besieged, took, destroyed, wasted, and
15 burned with fire; the inhabitants, young, old, male and
      female,
   horses, mules, asses, camels,
   oxen, and sheep without number I drove away and
   I made his land desolate, and diminished it.
Sisirtu and Kummakhlum, powerful
20 cities, together with the small cities of their environs,
   the land of Bit-Barru, in its entire extent,
   from his land I separated and to the
   land of Assyria added.   The city of Ilinzash
   I made the capital and fortress of that territory and
25 changed its former name;
   Kar-Sennacherib I named it.
   The people of the lands, the possession of my hands, I
      made to dwell there.
In the hands of my deputy, the governor of Kharkhar,[8]
I placed them, and widened my territory.   On my return
30 I received from the land of Media,[9] far away, of which
      land

---

[6] Hence the classical name of the district of Arrapakhitis, on the Upper Zab; now Albak.

[7] Ellipi was the country of which Ekbatana was subsequently the center, the Media of classical antiquity.

[8] Kharkhar adjoined Ellipi on the northeast.

[9] *Madai.* It must be remembered that the Medes spoken of by Sen-

no one of my fathers had heard the name,
a heavy tribute.
I placed them beneath the yoke of my lordship.
In my third campaign I marched to the land of the
    Hittites.[10]
35 Elulæus, King of Sidon, was overcome by the fear of
    the splendor
of my lordship and fled far away
to the sea and there made his abode.
Great Sidon, Little Sidon,
Bit-zitti, Sarepta, Makhalliba,
40 Ushu, Ekdippa, Akko,
his powerful cities, fortresses, pastures,
and cisterns, and his fortifications, the power of the
    arms
of Ashur, my lord, overcame and cast at
my feet. Ethobal upon the royal throne
45 I placed over them and a tribute of my lordship,
yearly and unchangeable, I set upon him.
Menahem of the city of Samsimuruna,
Ethobal of Sidon,
Abdili'ti of Arvad,
50 Urumilki of Byblos,
Mitinti of Ashdod,
Buduilu of Beth-Ammon,
Kammusu-nadab of Moab,
Malik-rammu of Edom,
55 all Kings of the west land,
brought rich presents, heavy gifts with merchandise,
before me, and kissed my feet.
And Tsidqa, the King of Ashkelon,
who had not submitted to my yoke, I brought out, the
    gods of the house of his fathers,

nacherib did not as yet inhabit the district of which Ekbatana subsequently became the capital. Hence the title of "far off," applied to
them here.
10 "The land of the Hittites" had now become a generic title, signi-
fying Syria generally. The Hittite kingdoms at Carchemish and else-
where had now ceased to exist.

THE ASSYRIANS ASSAULTING A CITY.

A sculptured slab of the Nimrod Palace. The advancing soldiers shoot from behind screens, an armored fort batters the wall, and impaled prisoners form the background.

60 himself, his wife, his sons, his daughters, his brothers,
the seed of the house of his fathers, and took them to
Assyria.
Sharru-ludari, the son of Rukibti, their former King,
I established over the people of Ashkelon; the giving of
tribute,
a present to my lordship, I put upon him, and he bears my
yoke.
65 In the course of my campaign Beth-Dagon,
Joppa, Benebarqa,[11] Azuru,
the cities of Tsidqa, which had not quickly
thrown themselves at my feet, I besieged, I took, I carried
away their spoil.
The governors, chiefs, and people of Ekron
70 who had cast Padi, their King according to Assyrian
right and oath,
into iron chains, and had, in hostile manner, given him
to Hezekiah of Judah — he shut him up in prison —
feared in their hearts. The kings of Egypt
called forth the archers, chariots, and horses of the King
of Melukhkhi,
75 a force without number, and came
to their help; before the city of Eltekeh
they arranged their battle array, appealing
to their weapons. With the help of Ashur, my lord,
I fought with them and accomplished their defeat.
80 The chief of the chariots and the sons of the King of
Egypt
and the chief of the chariots of the King of Melukhkhi my
hands
took alive in the fight. Eltekeh and
Timnath[12] I besieged, I took, and carried away their
spoil.

[11] The Beni-berak of Josh. xix. 45.
[12] See Gen. xxxviii. 12; Josh. xv. 10; Judg. xiv. 1, etc. The place is
now called Tibneh.

COLUMN III

To the city of Ekron I went; the governors
and princes, who had committed a transgression, I killed
and
bound their corpses on poles around the city.
The inhabitants of the city who had committed sin and evil
5 I counted as spoil; to the rest of them
who had committed no sin and wrong, who had
no guilt, I spoke peace. Padi,
their King, I brought forth from the
city of Jerusalem; upon the throne of lordship over them
10 I placed him. The tribute of my lordship
I laid upon him. But Hezekiah,
of Judah, who had not submitted to my yoke,
I besieged 46 of his strong cities, fortresses, and small
cities of their environs, without number, and
15 by casting down the walls and advancing the engines,
by an assault of the light-armed soldiers, by breaches, by
striking, and by axes
I took them; 200,150 men, young and old, male and
female,
horses, mules, asses, camels, oxen,
and sheep without number I brought out from them,
20 I counted them as spoil. Hezekiah himself I shut up
like a caged bird in Jerusalem,
his royal city; the walls I fortified
against him, and whosoever came out of the gates of the
city I turned
back. His cities, which I had plundered, I divided from
his land
and gave them to Mitinti, King of Ashdod,
25 to Padi, King of Ekron, and to Tsil-Bal,
King of Gaza, and thus diminished his territory.
To the former tribute, paid yearly,
I added the tribute of alliance of my lordship, and
laid that upon him. Hezekiah himself

30 was overwhelmed by the fear of the brightness of my lord-
    ship;
    the Arabians and his other faithful warriors
    whom, as a defense for Jerusalem, his royal city,
    he had brought in, fell into fear.
    With 30 talents of gold and 800 talents of silver, precious
        stones,
35 *gukhli daggassi,* large lapis lazuli,
    couches of ivory, thrones of ivory,
    ivory, *usu* wood, boxwood of every kind, a heavy trea-
        sure,
    and his daughters, his women of the palace,
    the young men and young women, to Nineveh, the city of
        my lordship,
40 I caused to be brought after me, and he sent his ambas-
        sadors
    to give tribute and to pay homage.
    In my fourth campaign Ashur my lord gave me confi-
        dence.
    I summoned my masses of troops; to the land of Bit-
        Yakin [13]
    I made them march.   In the course of my campaign
45 I accomplished at Bittutu the overthrow of
    Shuzub, the Chaldean, who dwelt in the marsh land.
    He was overcome by the fear of my battle-line,
    he lost heart, like a bird he fled alone,
    his trace was seen no more.   I turned about,
50 to the land of Bit-Yakin I took the road.
    Marduk-baladan, whose overthrow, in the course
    of my first campaign, I had accomplished and
    his power dispersed, feared the war-cry of my powerful
        arms
    and the advance of my strong battle-line, and
55 the gods who ruled his land he moved in their shrines, on
        ships
    he embarked them; to the city of Nagittu, in the swamps,

[13] The capital of Marduk-baladan, in the marshes in the south of
Babylonia.

by the sea-coast, he fled like a bird. His brothers, the
    seed of his fathers,
whom he left by the sea, together with the remaining
    people of this land,
from Bit-Yakin, marsh and meadow-land,
60 I brought them out, counted them slaves. I returned and
    destroyed his cities;
I wasted them, and made them like plowed land. Upon
    his confederate,
the King of Elam, I poured out fury.
On my return march I made Asur-nadin-sum, my first-
    born son,
the scion of my knees, sit upon the throne of his lordship
    and
65 the broad land of Sumer and Akkad I made subject to
    him.
In my fifth campaign the men of Tumurri,
Sarum, Isama, Kibsu, Khalbada,
Qua and Qana, whose dwellings, like the nest of the eagle
the king of birds, were located upon the pinnacle of
    Nippur,[14]
70 the steep mountain, had not yielded to my yoke.
At the foot of mount Nippur I placed my camp,
with my followers drawn up
and my unrelenting warriors,
I, like a strong wild ox, took the lead.
75 Clefts, ravines, mountain torrents, difficult high floods
in a chair I crossed, places impassable for the chair
I went down on foot, like an ibex I climbed to the high
    peaks
against them, wherever my knees
had a resting-place, I sat down on a rock;
80 waters of cold streams, for my thirst, I drank.
Upon the peaks of wooded mountains I pursued them,
I accomplished their destruction; their cities I took.

[14] Mount Taurus.

COLUMN IV

I took away their spoil, destroyed, wasted, and burned
     them with fire.
I turned about and against Maniae,
King of the city of Ukki, in the land of Daie, yet uncon-
     quered, I took the road.
Into the unopened path, the steep roads before
5 impassable mountains, before me
had no one of the former kings marched.
At the foot of Anara and Uppa, powerful mountains,
I placed my camp, and I, upon my chair,
with my unrelenting warriors,
10 entered, with weariness, into their narrow passes.
With difficulty I climbed the peaks of the steep mountains.
Maniae saw the dust of my soldiers'
feet, forsook Ukku, his royal city
and fled far away.   I besieged and took Ukku.
15 I took his spoil of all sorts, property and possessions;
the treasure of his palace I brought out
from it and counted as spoil, and 33
cities of the borders of his territory I took.   People, asses,
cattle and sheep I brought forth
20 from them.   I destroyed, wasted, and burned them with
     fire.
In my sixth campaign, the remaining inhabitants of Bit-
     Yakin
who had fled before my powerful arms, like
wild asses, and had moved the gods, who rule their lands,
in their shrines, and had crossed over the great sea
25 of the setting sun, and had set their homes in Nagitu,
of the land of Elam, therefore upon ships of the Hittites [15]
     I crossed the sea.
Nagitu, Nagitu-dibina, with Kilmu,
Pillatu and the land of Khupapanu, districts
of the land of Elam I took.   The people of Bit-Yakin,
     with their gods,

[15] That is, Syrians.

30 and the people of the King of Elam I took, and left behind
   no settler.
   In ships I brought them; over to the coast
   on this side I made them cross and take the road to
   Assyria.
   The cities of those districts I destroyed, wasted,
   burned with fire and made them heaps and plowed land.
35 On my return Shuzub, of Babylon,
   who, through an attack on the land, had seized
   the lordship of Sumer and Akkad, in open battle
   I defeated, I took him alive with my own hand,
   in fetters and bands of iron I put him, and to Assyria
40 I brought him.   The King of Elam, who had helped him
   and marched to his aid, I overcame;
   his power I scattered, I broke down his army.
   In my seventh campaign Ashur my lord gave me confidence.
   To the land of Elam I marched.   Bit-Khairi
45 and Rasa, cities of the Assyrian territory
   which, in the reign of my fathers, the Elamites had torn
   away by force,
   In the course of my campaign I took, and seized their
   spoil.
   My royal warriors I took into them.
   To the territory of Assyria I returned them and
50 gave them into the hands of the chief of Khaltsu dur-sami-
   irtsiti.
   The cities of Bubi, Dunnisamas, Bit-risia,
   Bit-uklame, Duru, Danti-Sulai,
   Siliptu, Bit-asusi, Karmubasa,
   Bit-gissi, Bit-kappalani, Bit-imbia,
55 Khamanu, Bit-arrabi, Burutu,
   Dintu-sa-Sulai, Dintu-
   sa-Turbititir, Kharriaslaki, Rabai,
   Rasu, Akkabarina, Tilukhuri,
   Khamranu, Naditu, with the cities at the entrance
60 toward Bit-bunaki, Til-khumbi, Dintu-sa-
   Dumean, Bit-ubia, Baltilisir,

Tagallisir, Sanakidati,
Masutu-saplitu, Sarkhuderi, Alum-sa-tarbit,
Bit-akhiddina, Ilteuba, 34 powerful cities
65 and the smaller cities in their environs
without number, I besieged, took, and carried off their
spoil,
I destroyed, wasted, and burned them with fire.
With the smoke of their burning, like a dark cloud
I covered the face of the broad heaven.   When Kudur-
Nakhundu,
70 the Elamite, heard of the taking of his cities, fear
overcame him.   He made his remaining cities fortresses.
He left Madakti, his royal city, and
to Khaidala, which is among the far-away mountains,
took his way.   To Madakti, his royal city,
75 I ordered the march.   In the month Tebet, a great cold
set in, the heaven poured down rain,
rain upon rain and snow; streams and torrents
from mountains I feared.   I turned about and
took the road to Nineveh.   In those days,
80 by command of Ashur my lord, Kudur-Nakhundi,

COLUMN V

the King of Elam, did not live three months.
On a day not destined for him he died suddenly.
After him Ummam-minanu, without judgment and intel-
ligence,
his younger brother, set himself on his throne.
5 In my eighth campaign, after Suzub had been carried off,
and the people of Babylon, evil devils had closed their
city gates,
their heart planned the making of a rebellion.
Around Suzub, the Chaldean, the wicked, the base,
who has no strength, a vassal under the control of the
governor
10 of Lakhiru, the fugitive, the deserter,
the bloodthirsty, they gathered and
marched into the marsh-land and made a revolt.

I surrounded them with an army and threatened his life.
On account of terror and distress he fled to Elam.

15 As infamy and wrong were around him
he hastened from Elam and entered Babylon.
The Babylonians illegitimately set him on
the throne, and the lordship of Sumer and Akkad entrusted to him.
The treasure-house of E-saggil they opened, and the gold
and silver

20 of Bel and Zarbanit, which they brought from their tem-
ples,
they gave as a bribe to Umman-minanu, the King of Elam,
who was without
judgment and insight, saying to him:
"Assemble thy army, gather thy forces,
hasten to Babylon, help us,

25 our confidence art thou."   He, the Elamite,
whose cities, in the course of my former campaign
against Elam I had taken, and turned into plow-land,
took no thought, he received the bribe from them and
assembled his soldiers and forces; his chariots and bag-
gage-wagons

30 he brought together, horses and mules he placed in spans.
The lands of Parsuas, Anzan, Pasiru, Ellipi,
Iazan, Lagabra, Karzunu,
Dumuqu, Sulai, Samunu,
the son of Marduk-baladan, Bit-adini, Bit-amukkana,

35 Bit-sillana, Bit-saludadakki, Lakhiru,
the Puqudu, the Gambulum, the Khalatu, the Ruua,
the Ubulum, the Malakhu, the Rapiqu,
the Khindaru, the Damunu, a great confederation,
he called unto him.   Their great throng took the

40 road to Akkad and came to Babylon.
Together with Suzub the Chaldean, King of Babylon,
they made an alliance and united their forces,
like a great swarm of locusts, on the surface of the earth;
together, they came to do battle

45 against me.   The dust of their feet was like a storm

by which the wide heavens are covered with
thick clouds.   Before me in the city of Khaluli,
on the banks of the Tigris, the line of battle was drawn up.
Before me they stationed themselves, they brandished
    their arms.
50 I prayed to Ashur, Sin, Shamash, Bel, Nabu, Nergal,
Ishtar of Nineveh, Ishtar of Arbela, the gods of my con-
    fidence,
to overcome my powerful enemy.
My prayers they quickly heard, they came
to my help.   Like a lion I raged and put on
55 my cuirass and with my helmet, sign of war,
I covered my head.   Into my high war-chariot,
which wipes out the refractory, with the fury of my heart
I climbed quickly.   The powerful bow,
which Ashur had entrusted to me, I seized,
60 the javelin which destroys life I seized with my hand.
Against all the troops, evil enemies,
oppressed, I roared like a lion, like Ramman I raged.
At the command of Ashur, the great lord, my lord, on
    flank and front,
like the advance of a wild flood, upon the enemy I fell.
65 With the confidence of Ashur, and the advance of my
    powerful
line of battle, I struck their front and brought about
their retreat.   The hostile forces with arrow and lance
I destroyed, through the mass of their corpses I cleared
    my way.
Khumba-nudasa, chief
70 of the King of Elam, a careful champion, who ruled
his troops, in whom he had great confidence, him,
    together with his chief men,
whose girdle-dagger was embossed with gold, and whose
    wrists
were bound with double bracelets of shining gold,
like fat steers, laid in chains,
75 I quickly destroyed, and accomplished their defeat.
Their necks I cut off like lambs,

their precious lives I cut through like a knot;
like a heavy rain, their trophies and arms
I scattered over the wide field.

80 The chargers of my chariot
swam in the masses of blood as in a river,
crushing evil and bad;
blood and filth ran down its wheel.
With the corpses of their warriors, as with herbs
I filled the field.   I cut off their testicles.

COLUMN VI

Their pudenda I tore from them like the seed of
cucumbers.   I cut off their hands.
The bracelets of gold and silver, which were on their
    arms, I took off.
With sharp swords I cut off their noses.

5 The gold and silver girdle-daggers, which they carried, I
    took away.
The rest of his officers, and Nabu-sum-iskun,
the son of Marduk-baladan, who feared
my line of battle, but had gone with them, in the midst
of the battle I seized them alive, with my hands.   Their
    chariots

10 with their horses, whose drivers, in the onset of battle,
had been killed, while they were left
and went up and down by themselves,
these I turned together.   Until the fourth hour of the
    night it went on.
Then I stopped their slaughter.   Umman-minanu,

15 King of Elam, together with the King of Babylon, the
    princes
of Chaldea, who had helped them, the vehemence of my
    battle-line, like a bull
overwhelmed them.   They left their tents.
To save their lives they trampled over the bodies of
their soldiers and fled.   Like young captured birds they
    lost courage.

20 With their urine they defiled their chariots

and let fall their excrement.   To pursue them
I sent my chariots and horses after them.
Their fugitives, who had gone out to save their lives
wherever they were overtaken, were thrown down by
    arms.
25 In those days, after I had finished the palace adjoining
    the wall of
Nineveh for a royal dwelling, and
to the astonishment of all people had adorned it;
the side building, for keeping in order the train,
for the keeping of horses, and all sorts of things
30 which the kings, my forefathers and fathers, had built,
it had no foundation, its room was too small,
the workmanship was not tasteful.   In the course of
    time, its base
had become weak, the part under ground had given way,
    and the upper part was in ruins.
That palace I tore down completely.
35 A great mass of building-material I took out of the
    ground.
The surrounding part of the city I cut off and added
to it.   The place of the old palace I left.
With earth from the river-bed I filled it up.
The lower ground I raised 200 *tipki*
40 above the level.   In a favorable month
on an auspicious day I built on this foundation according
    to the wisdom of my heart
a palace of *pilu* stone and cedar-wood, in the style
of the Hittites, and a great palace in the Assyrian style,
which far exceeded the former in adaptation,
45 size, and artistic excellence, through the work of the
wise builders of my royal rule.
Great cedar-beams from Khamanu,[16]
a snow-capped mountain, I brought hither.
The doors of *liari* wood I surrounded with a cover
50 of gleaming bronze, and I put in the doors.
With white *pilu* stones, which were found in the

[16] Mount Amanus.

environs of Buladai, I made great bull colossi
and placed them by the doors on the left and
right.   For the equipment of the black-headed men, for
    the receiving
55 of horses, mules, calves, asses,
chariots, bow-strings, quivers,
bows and arrows, every sort of tool for war,
the harness for horses and mules,
which have great power when yoked,
60 I made rooms and greatly enlarged them.
I built that palace from foundation to roof
and finished it.   My inscription
I brought into it.   For future days,
whoever — among the kings, my successors, whom Ashur
    and Ishtar
65 shall call to rule over the land and people —
the prince may be, if this palace
becomes old and ruined, who builds it anew
may he preserve my inscription,
anoint it with oil, offer sacrifices, return it to its place;
70 then will Ashur and Ishtar hear his prayer.
·Whoever alters my writing and name
him may Ashur, the great lord, the father of gods, afflict
    like an enemy
and take scepter and throne from him and destroy his rule.
Dated the month Adar of the archonate of Bel-imurani,
75 prefect of Carchemish.

This is the end of this publication.

Any remaining blank pages are for our book binding
requirements and are blank on purpose.

To search thousands of interesting publications like this one,
please remember to visit our website at:

http://www.kessinger.net

CPSIA information can be obtained at www.ICGtesting.com
Printed in the USA
LVOW131625270312

275001LV00011B/2/P